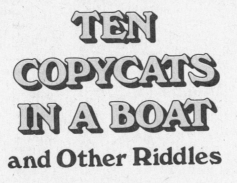

TEN COPYCATS IN A BOAT

and Other Riddles

Weekly Reader Books presents

An I CAN READ Book

TEN COPYCATS IN A BOAT

and Other Riddles

by ALVIN SCHWARTZ

Pictures by
MARC SIMONT

Harper & Row, Publishers

This book is a presentation of Weekly Reader Books.
Weekly Reader Books offers book clubs for children from
preschool through junior high school.

For further information write to:
Weekly Reader Books
1250 Fairwood Ave.
Columbus, Ohio 43216

Ten Copycats in a Boat and Other Riddles
Text copyright © 1980 by Alvin Schwartz
Illustrations copyright © 1980 by Marc Simont
Printed in
the United States of America. For information address
Harper & Row, Publishers, Inc., 10 East 53rd Street,
New York, N.Y. 10022. Published simultaneously in
Canada by Fitzhenry & Whiteside Limited, Toronto.
FIRST EDITION

Library of Congress Cataloging in Publication Data
Main entry under title: ⁻
Ten copycats in a boat, and other riddles.

(An I can read book)
SUMMARY: A collection of riddles selected from
folklore around the world.
1. Riddles—Juvenile literature.
[1. Riddles. 2. Folklore] I. Schwartz, Alvin,
date   II. Simont, Marc.
PN6371.5.T4   398'.6   79-2811
ISBN 0-06-025237-5
ISBN 0-06-025238-3 (lib. bdg.)

Weekly Reader Books offers several exciting
card and activity programs. For information,
write to WEEKLY READER BOOKS, P.O. Box 16636,
Columbus, Ohio 43216.

Ten copycats were sitting in a boat,

and one jumped out.

How many were left?

None. They all were copycats.

What does a cat have

that no other animal has?

Kittens.

If you put four ducks in a box,

what would you have?

A box of quackers.

What has two heads, four eyes,

six legs, and a tail?

A horse and a rider.

What is

over your head

and under your hat?

Your hair.

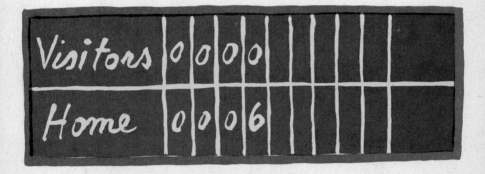

A baseball team scored six runs

in one inning,

but not one man reached home.

Why not?

It was a girls' team.

If you threw a white stone

into the Red Sea,

what would it become?

17

Wet.

What gets wetter and wetter

the more it dries?

19

A towel.

How many letters are there in
the alphabet?

Eleven.

The ALPHABET

"Never use the letter D."

"Why not?"

"It makes Ma mad."

What word does everybody say wrong?

Wrong!

What is the longest word

in the world?

SMILES.

There is a mile

between the first letter

and the last letter.

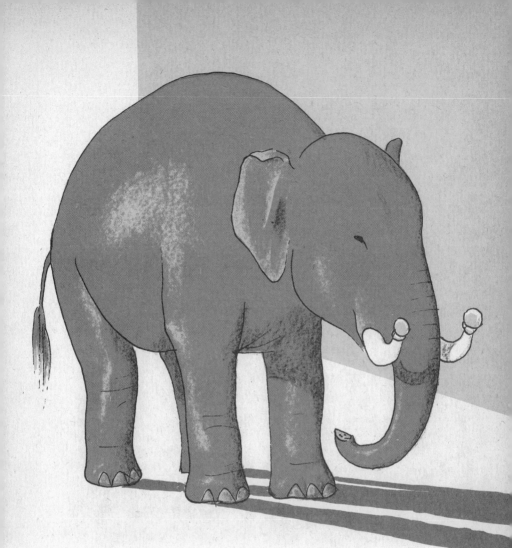

What is as big as an elephant,
but weighs nothing at all?

The shadow of an elephant.

Why do dragons sleep all day?

31

They like to hunt knights.

What always sleeps

with its shoes on?

A horse.

"What is yellow and brown
and has a hundred legs?"
"I don't know."
"I don't know either, but…

it is crawling up your neck!"

Why shouldn't you tell secrets
on a farm?

The corn has ears.

The potatoes have eyes.

And the beanstalk.

What did the pig say

when the farmer grabbed its tail?

That is the end of me!

An eagle flew through the sky,

and a dog sat on its tail.

How could that be?

What is the best way

to catch a squirrel?

43

Climb into a tree

and act like a nut.

What is this a picture of?

Snow White in a snowstorm.

S	M	T	W	T	F	S
			1	2	3	4
5	6	7	8	9	10	11
12	13	14	15	16	17	18
19	20	21	22	23	24	25
26	27	28	29	30		

Where does Friday

come before Thursday?

In a dictionary.

When is a car not a car?

When it turns into

a parking lot.

How many sides

has a glass of lemonade?

Two—the inside and the outside.

What is the difference

between a jeweler

and a jailer?

53

A jeweler sells watches.

A jailer watches cells.

What invention

lets you look

right through a wall?

A window.

A boy fell off

a hundred-foot ladder.

But he did not get hurt.

Why didn't he?

He fell off the bottom step.

58

A girl dreamed

a lion was chasing her.

He was getting closer and closer.

Then she came to a tall tree.

And to escape

she climbed all the way

to the top.

But at the top

she found a giant snake.

So there she was

with a snake in the tree

and a lion on the ground.

How did she get away?

She woke up.

There are millions of riddles to tell.
Some are puzzles that make you think
good and hard. Others are jokes and tricks
that make you laugh good and hard.

They are found everywhere. Yet each was
created by an unknown person.

Many of these riddles are very old. The
riddle about a "monster" with two heads, on
page 11, is an example. It was used by some
children in England over three hundred
years ago.

Since then this riddle has traveled to
many places, including the place where
you live.